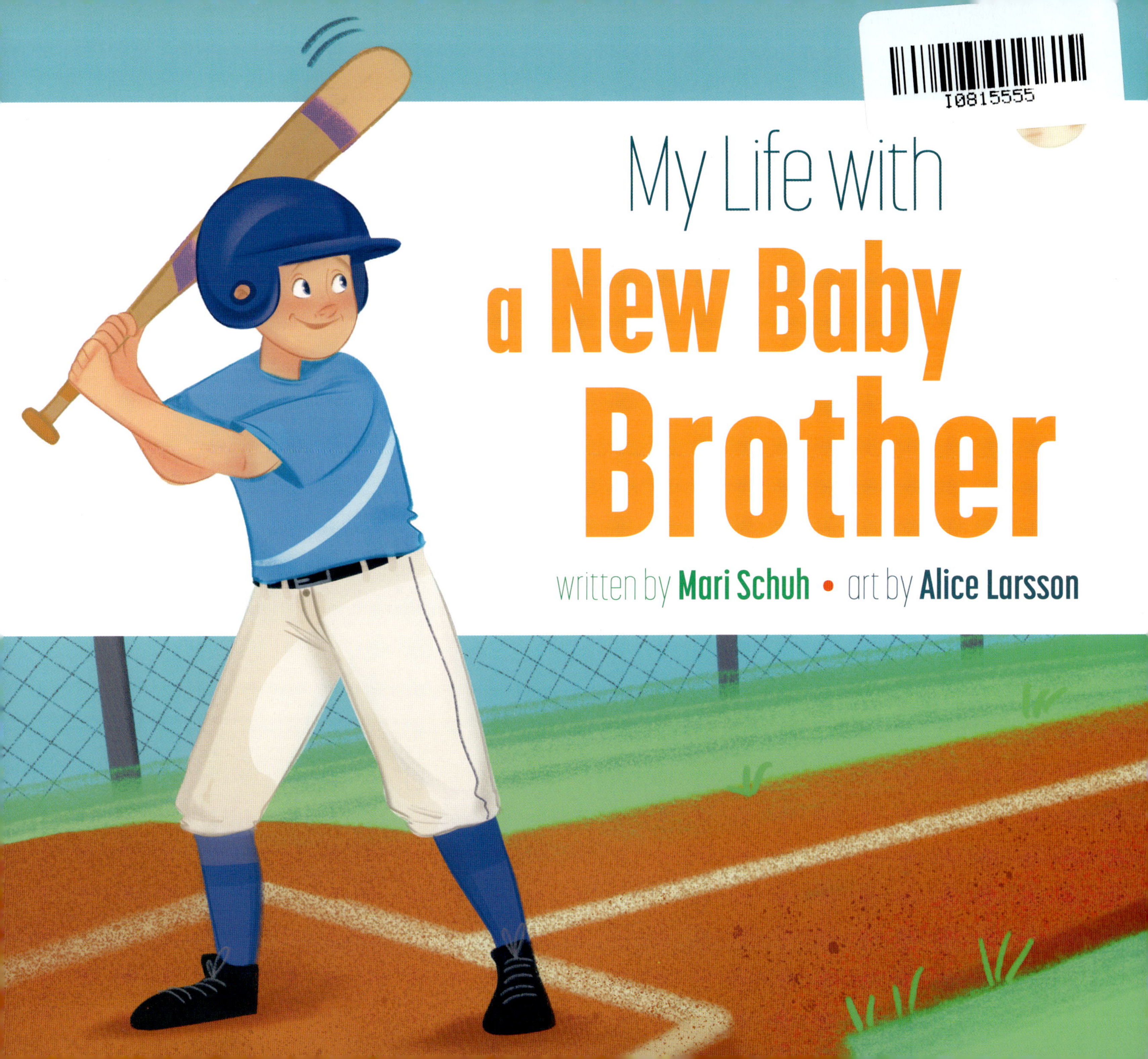

My Life with a New Baby Brother

written by Mari Schuh • art by Alice Larsson

I0815555

AMICUS ILLUSTRATED
is published by Amicus Learning, an imprint of Amicus
P.O. Box 227, Mankato, MN 56002
www.amicuspublishing.us

Copyright © 2026 Amicus. International copyright reserved in all countries. No part of this book may be reproduced in any form without written permission from the publisher.

Editor: Rebecca Glaser
Series Designer: Kathleen Petelinsek
Book Designer: Emily Dietz

Cataloging-in-Publication data is available from the Library of Congress

Library Binding ISBN: 9798892008877
Paperback ISBN: 9798892009539
eBook ISBN: 9798896850199

LCCN: 2025014230

Printed in China

About the Author
Mari Schuh's love of reading began with cereal boxes at the kitchen table. Today she is the author of hundreds of nonfiction books for beginning readers. With each book, Mari hopes she's helping kids learn a little bit more about the world around them. Find out more about her at marischuh.com.

About the Illustrator
Alice Larsson is a London-based illustrator originally from Sweden. A natural creative, she is thrilled to be able to connect characters and stories through her work. Outside of drawing, Alice loves spending time with family and friends, as well as reading books and traveling, which sparks her creativity.

Hi! My name is Kane. We might like some of the same things. I like to read and play sports. Our families might be different. I have one younger brother. Let me tell you about my life.

For a long time I was an only child. Then when I was six, my parents surprised me. They gave me a shirt that said, "I am a big brother." I was so happy!

I had wanted a brother or sister for a long time. Playing by myself made me lonely. I tried to make one of our dogs play soccer with me. But he wasn't very good.

I was excited to meet the new baby. But I had to be patient. I had to wait for months and months. Mom's belly got bigger. One day when I touched her belly, I felt the baby kick! At the doctor's office, I got to hear the baby's heartbeat.

When he was finally born, I felt excited and nervous. I got to hold him and cuddle him. My mom and dad named him Briggs. We all loved him right away.

When Briggs was a newborn, I couldn't play with him just yet. But he could go to my games. He went to my basketball game when he was three days old!

I waited for Briggs to grow. Now he is one and a half years old. We have fun playing together. I taught him how to say the word brother.

Having a little brother is great. But it can also be hard. When we go shopping with Briggs, he screams a lot. He grabs items off the shelves.

Briggs started walking when he was about one year old. This makes it harder for me to do homework. He often grabs my papers and runs away. He thinks it's funny! But I don't.

My family likes to play board games. But Briggs sometimes breaks the game board. He also takes the game pieces. So sometimes we wait until he goes to sleep. Then I play with just my mom and dad.

I am more responsible now. I remember to lock my bedroom door. Briggs tries to get into my bedroom. He wants to play with my toys. But he might break them.

I try to be patient, too. Mom usually has to help Briggs first. He is not patient. At meals, Mom feeds Briggs first. At night, Mom puts Briggs to bed first. I wait for my turn.

I love my brother very much. When he cries, I can make him smile and laugh. When Mom is busy, I make sure he stays safe. He loves me, too! When Mom and I pick him up from daycare, he runs to me first.

It’s fun to watch Briggs grow and learn. He can kick and throw a ball to me. But he can’t catch a ball yet. I can’t wait until he gets older. Then we can play sports together. It will be lots of fun!

Meet Kane

Hello! I'm Kane. I live in Minnesota with my family. We have four dogs. Their names are Kobe, Cal, Gio, and Chris. My favorite color is blue. I like to eat pizza, shrimp, and tri-tip steak. I enjoy reading action books. Writing is also fun. I have a big imagination. When I grow up, I want to be a writer.

Respecting Families with a New Baby

Getting a new sibling is a big change. Be kind and understanding.

Your friend with a new baby brother or sister might not always be able to play with you. They might be spending time with the new baby or helping their parents.

If you are sick, it's best not to visit babies. You could make them sick, too.

Babies are cute and often get a lot of attention. An older sibling may feel left out. You can spend time with them.

If your family brings a gift for a new baby, bring a small gift for older siblings too. Then they won't feel left out.

No two families are the same. Each family has its own activities, rules, and traditions. Respect your friend's family.

Helpful Terms

nervous Being worried or fearful.

newborn A baby who was just born, usually about 0 to 3 months old.

patient Being calm while waiting for something.

responsible Able to keep promises, follow rules, and do what you say you will do.

sibling A brother or a sister. Full siblings have the same mom and dad.

Read More

Chevallerau, Manon. ***You're Going to Be a Big Sibling.*** New York: Odd Dot, an imprint of Macmillan, 2024.

Finne, Stephanie. ***Siblings.*** Minneapolis: Jump!, Inc., 2025.

Reagan, Jean. ***How to Welcome a New Baby.*** New York: Knopf Books for Young Readers, 2022.

Websites

KIDSHEALTH: TALKING ABOUT YOUR FEELINGS

https://kidshealth.org/en/kids/talk-feelings.html

Kids can have many feelings about a new sibling. Read this helpful website for ways to talk about your feelings.

PBS KIDS CELEBRATES: SIBLINGS DAY

https://www.youtube.com/shorts/-JluKcPrMCw

Enjoy this short video celebrating siblings.

SESAME WORKSHOP: GETTING ALONG WITH SIBLINGS

https://sesameworkshop.org/resources/getting-along-siblings/

Visit this website to watch a video about how siblings can get along with one another.

Every effort has been made to ensure that these websites are appropriate for children. However, because of the nature of the Internet, it is impossible to guarantee that these sites will remain active indefinitely or that their contents will not be altered.